ISBN: 1-57051-418-6

Cover/Interior:
Koechel Peterson & Associates

Concept, art direction and lettering:
Joanne Fink

Printed in USA

A Special Gift

For

_____

With Love From

_____

Date

_____

Introduction

It has been said that the greatest gift
one may give to another is the gift of love.
Whether it is soft and comfortable as an easy chair,
or as romantic and tender as a first kiss,
it is the essence of all that is good.

'With All My Heart' captures some of the magic
of a loving relationship through inspirational
quotes on love, togetherness, sharing, romance,
and friendship. It is an ideal gift to share with
the person that you love the most.

With all My Heart

Illustrated by
Joyce Shelton

Compiled by
RosaLinda Buchner
Graziano

Brownlow

Love

LOVE is patient and kind;

Love bears all things,

believes all things,

hopes all things,

endures all things,

Love never fails.

So faith, hope, love abide,

these three;

but the greatest of these

is LOVE.

-1 Corinthians 13:4-8,13

Where there is great love, there are always miracles.

-WILLA CATHER

Where your pleasure is, there is your treasure;

where your treasure, there your heart;

where your heart, there your happiness.

-AUGUSTINE

When we reflect on the meaning of love,

we see that it is to the heart what the summer

is to the farmer's year. It brings to harvest all

the loveliest flowers of the soul.

-BILLY GRAHAM

Beloved, let us love one another: for love is of God.

-1 John 4:7

Those who love deeply never grow old;

they may die of old age, but they die young.

-Arthur W. Pinero

Love is never satisfied with doing or giving

anything but the heart.

-J. M. Gibbon

Two souls with but a single thought;

Two hearts that beat as one.

-Von Munch Bellinghausen

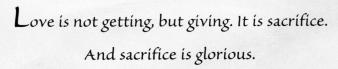

Love is not getting, but giving. It is sacrifice.

And sacrifice is glorious.

-JOANA FIELD

Love each other deeply with all your heart.

-1 PETER 1:22

When I have learned to love God better

than my earthly dearest, I shall love my earthly

dearest better than I do now.

-C.S. LEWIS

Where love is concerned,

too much is not even enough!

-DE BEAUMARCHAIS

I Love You

I Love You not only for what you are,
but for what I am when I am with you.
I love you not only for what you
have made of yourself,
but for the part of me that you bring out.

I Love You for putting your hand
into my heaped up heart,
and passing over all the foolish and
frivolous and weak things which you
cannot help dimly seeing there,
and for drawing out into the light
all the beautiful, radiant things
that no one else had looked
quite far enough to find.

I Love You for ignoring the possibilities
of the fool and weakling in me,
and for laying firm hold on
the possibilities of good in me.

I Love You because you are helping
me to make of the lumber of my life
not a tavern but a temple,
and of the words of my every day
not a reproach but a song.

I Love You because you have done more than
any creed could have done to make me good,
and more than any fate could have done
to make me happy.
You have done it just by being yourself.

-ROY CROFT

Togetherness

Love does not consist

in gazing at each other,

but in looking outward

together

in the same direction.

-ANTOINE DE SAINT-EXUPERY

Whither thou goest, I will go;

and where thou lodgest, I will lodge; thy people

shall be my people, and thy God my God.

- RUTH 1:16

Two such as you with such a master speed

Cannot be parted nor swept away

From one another once you are agreed

That life is only life forevermore

Together wing to wing, and oar to oar.

- ROBERT FROST

Weave the threads of your

lives together with Love.

- JOANNE FINK

Couples in love are like coals in a fire.
When they stay close together, they remain bright
and alive. When they move apart, they die.

-PAUL C. BROWNLOW

I like not only to be loved,

but to be told I am loved.

-GEORGE ELIOT

Two hearts are better than one.

If one falls down,

his companion can help him up.

But pity the person who has

no companion to help him up.

-ECCLESIASTES 4:9-10 (paraphrase)

As you walk down life's path together,

share your thoughts and unite your spirits in love.

-JOANNE FINK

Love is the touch of your hand in mine.

-ROSALINDA BUCHNER GRAZIANO

There is no more lovely,

friendly and charming relationship,

communion or company

than a good marriage.

-MARTIN LUTHER

Not Two, But One

Now you will feel no rain,
for each of you
will be shelter for the other.

Now you will feel no cold,
for each of you
will be warmth for the other.

Now there is no more loneliness.

Now you are two persons,
but there is only one life before you.
May your days together
be good and long
upon the earth.

-Apache Marriage Blessing

How great is God's goodness
to have given you to me to love for a lifetime.

-ANONYMOUS

Love alone is capable of uniting living beings
in such a way as to complete and fulfill them,
for it alone takes them and joins them
by what is deepest in themselves.

-PIERRE TEILHARD DE CHARDIN

Let love be your greatest aim.

-1 CORINTHIANS 14:1

The great tragedy of life is not that men perish,
but that they cease to love.

-W. SOMERSET MAUGHAM

Sharing

Only when you share

the dreams in your heart;

Only when you unlock

the secrets of your soul;

Only when you give

sincerely and honestly

of yourself to each other...

will you then know

the meaning of True Love.

-RosaLinda Buchner Graziano

It was good of you to share in my troubles.

In the early days of our acquaintance, no one shared

with me in giving and receiving except you only.

-Philippians 4:14,15 (paraphrase)

May the love you share be as timeless

as the tides and as deep as the sea.

-Anonymous

Hearts that share one Love, one Life,

will always know true Joy.

-Jason Blake

Every meal shared in love is a feast.

-Proverb

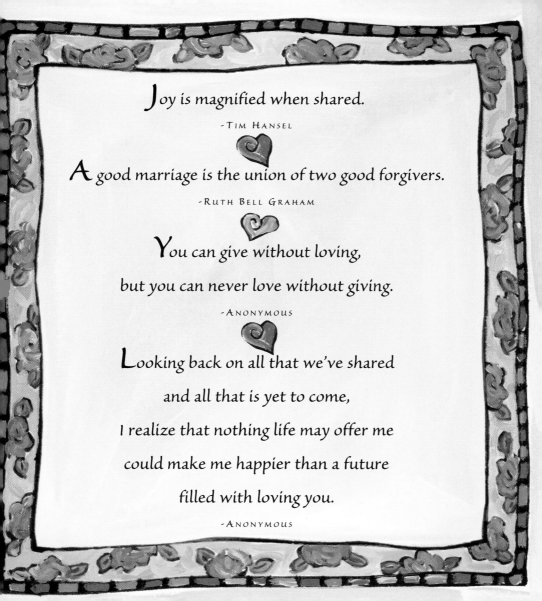

Joy is magnified when shared.

-TIM HANSEL

A good marriage is the union of two good forgivers.

-RUTH BELL GRAHAM

You can give without loving,

but you can never love without giving.

-ANONYMOUS

Looking back on all that we've shared

and all that is yet to come,

I realize that nothing life may offer me

could make me happier than a future

filled with loving you.

-ANONYMOUS

I Promise to Share

I promise to share with you in times of joy

as in times of trouble; To talk and to listen;

To honor and to appreciate you; To provide

for and support you in Trust and in Love.

It is rare to find a person who not only

accepts you for what you are, but also

makes you feel good about

being yourself.

I want to thank you for helping me find

the best part of who I am, and for letting

me share it with you.

I appreciate your love, wisdom and understanding.

I promise to share my hopes, thoughts

and dreams with you.

I promise to treasure the wonderful,

unique person that you are.

When we are together,

nothing seems impossible.

I love you very much.

-JOANNE FINK

Romance

Love is the music
you bring to my heart;
and the song it sings
to my soul.

-RosaLinda Buchner Graziano

My heart is ever at your service.

-SHAKESPEARE

I wish I could tell you the day,

the hour, the minute

my love for you became real.

I only know it seems

I've loved you forever.

-ANONYMOUS

Night and day you are the one,

Only you beneath the moon

and under the sun.

-COLE PORTER

A Season of Singing

See! The winter is past;

the rains are over and gone.

Flowers appear on the earth;

the season of singing has come,

the cooing of doves is heard in our land.

The fig tree forms its early fruit;

the blossoming vines spread their fragrance.

Arise, come, my darling;

My beautiful one, come with me.

–SONG OF SOLOMON 2:11-13

I love you, not because you're perfect,

but because you are so absolutely perfect for me.

-ANONYMOUS

Affection is responsible for nine-tenths

of whatever solid and durable happiness

there is in our natural lives.

-C. S. LEWIS

Love puts the fun in together,

the sad in apart,

the hope in tomorrow,

the joy in a heart.

-ANONYMOUS

How do I love Thee?

How do I love thee?

Let me count the ways.

I love thee to the depth

and breadth and height

My soul can reach,

when feeling out of sight

For the ends of Being and ideal Grace.

I love thee to the level of every day's

most quiet need,

by sun and candle-light.

I love thee freely,

    as men strive for Right;

I love thee purely,

    as they turn from Praise.

I love thee with the passion put to use

In my old griefs,

    and with my childhood's faith.

I love thee with a love

    I seemed to lose

With my lost saints;

    I love thee with the breath,

    Smiles, tears, of all my life!

and, if God choose,

I shall but love thee better after death.

-Elizabeth Barrett Browning

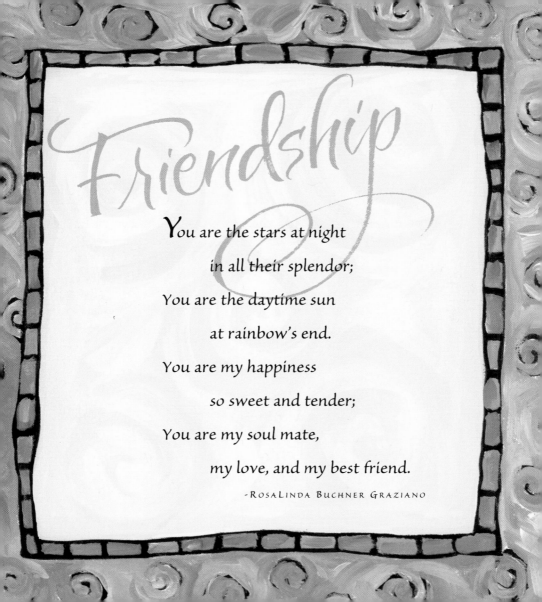

Friendship

You are the stars at night

in all their splendor;

You are the daytime sun

at rainbow's end.

You are my happiness

so sweet and tender;

You are my soul mate,

my love, and my best friend.

-ROSALINDA BUCHNER GRAZIANO

If human love does not carry a man beyond himself,

it is not love. If love is always discreet, always wise, always

sensible and calculating, never carried beyond itself,

it is not love at all. It may be affection, it may be warmth

of feeling, but it has not the true nature of love in it.

-Oswald Chambers

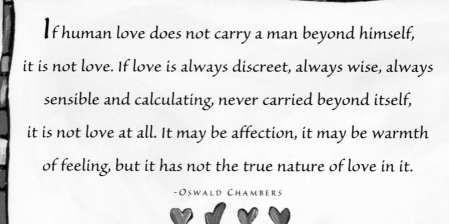

A friend is someone who not only

accepts you for what you are,

but makes you feel good about being yourself.

-Joanne Fink

The fingers of God touch your life

when you touch a friend.

-Mary Dawn Hughes

No love, no friendship

can cross the path

of our destiny without leaving

some mark on it forever.

-FRANCOIS MAURIAC

Having someone with whom

to laugh, talk, cry and dream,

is having a friend to love.

-JOANNE FINK

Real friends have a great time

doing absolutely nothing together.

-ANONYMOUS

The roots of friendship grow deep
when planted and nurtured with care,
tended and tilled with affection,
and showered with love and prayer.

-ROSALINDA BUCHNER GRAZIANO

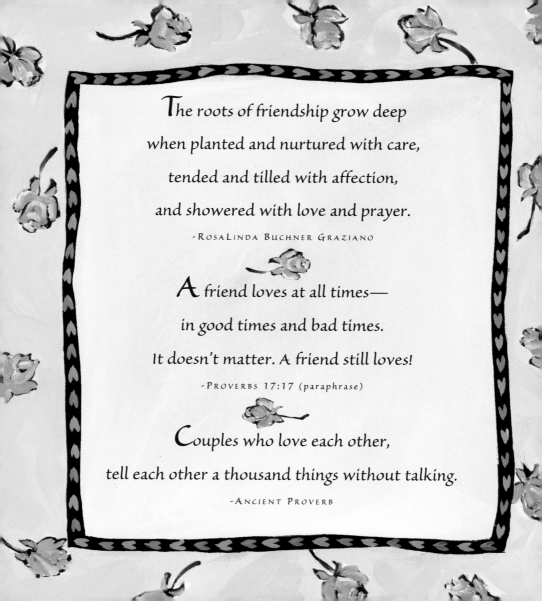

A friend loves at all times—

in good times and bad times.

It doesn't matter. A friend still loves!

-PROVERBS 17:17 (paraphrase)

Couples who love each other,

tell each other a thousand things without talking.

-ANCIENT PROVERB

Friendship is the comfort,

the inexpressible comfort

of feeling safe with another person,

having neither to weigh thoughts

nor measure words,

but pouring them all right out

just as they are,

chaff and grain together,

certain that a faithful friendly hand

will take and sift them;

keep what is worth keeping,

and with a breath of comfort

blow the rest away.

-DINAH MARIA MULOCK CRAIK

Plant a word of love heart-deep in a person's life.

Nurture it with a smile and a prayer,

and watch what happens.

-MAX LUCADO

Let love and faithfulness never leave you;

bind them around your neck,

write them on the tablet of your heart.

-PROVERBS 3:3

One hundred years together

Would surely be too few,

For every day, all over again,

I fall in love with you.

-ANONYMOUS